T0157521

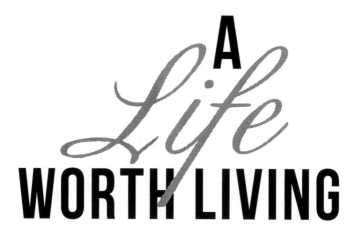

A *Life* WORTH LIVING

RYAN YELLOWLEES
EDITED BY GREG BAKER

WESTBOW
PRESS®
A DIVISION OF THOMAS NELSON
& ZONDERVAN

WestBow Press books may be ordered through booksellers or by contacting:

WestBow Press
A Division of Thomas Nelson & Zondervan
1663 Liberty Drive
Bloomington, IN 47403
www.westbowpress.com
844-714-3454

ISBN: 979-8-3850-0817-9 (sc)
ISBN: 979-8-3850-0818-6 (e)

Library of Congress Control Number: 2023917939

Print information available on the last page.

WestBow Press rev. date: 11/07/2023

INTRODUCTION

My name is Ryan James Yellowlees. I want to share my story of finding extraordinary love, joy, fulfilment, meaning, purpose, and redemption, turning great adversity into a great victory, impossibility into possibility, hopelessness into hopefulness, sorrow into joy, and darkness into light. My story is a testimony that you can have a great life worth living no matter who you are and regardless of your circumstances. My story is also an example of how you can have a transformed, powerful life filled with purpose and meaning.

I cannot deny that life has moments of heartache and pain, but we cannot experience joy without pain. Without sadness and sorrow, joy would have no meaning. Pain is a great teacher; it gives us knowledge and understanding that matures us into who we are. Sometimes, we find ourselves in seemingly impossible seasons, making us feel trapped and full of anxiety, despair, and hopelessness. I want to encourage you that there is hope in impossible situations. I have had more than my share of them that turned into great victories beyond my imagination.

I was born with Duchenne muscular dystrophy, a progressive genetic illness that causes all the muscles in the body to break down. It is eventually fatal. However, I can say that my life is full of purpose, meaning...a life worth living. Being born with this illness was a tragedy that turned into a blessing.

If I could go back and choose to be born without this illness, I would not.

This illness made me who I am, and with out it, I would not have gotten to know all the wonderful people in my life. Life is too short, so I want to live it to the fullest and die without regrets. I do not want to waste time on engaging in self-pity, feeling sorry for myself, or giving up in defeat. Life is a beautiful gift that we often take for granted or do not appreciate.

Chapter 1

STUMBLING IN DARKNESS

My life before I met Jesus, my Lord and personal Saviour and Friend, was the most painful season of my existence. My life without Jesus was not worth living, had no purpose, and was surrounded by unbearable darkness, but God did not want that for me. God gave me my middle name of James, which has great significance. James has the same meaning as Jacob, which means "a substitute, to replace, or may God protect." Having the name James is a prophecy that illustrates the love of Jesus, who is our substitute for our sins when He died on the cross for us. More than that, my life shows we all can have a personal relationship with God. The other prophetic meaning of James is the blessing "may God protect," which is exactly what happened to me. God protected me from the brink of death multiple times, a fact that continues to baffled many doctors.

I was born into a non-Christian (no relationship with Jesus) family in May of 1993 in British Columbia, Canada. When I was born, I was considered a healthy baby boy. My family became mildly concerned about my health when I started walking at seventeen months old, which is considered late. As time passed, my maternal grandmother became increasingly concerned about my health because I had great difficulty walking and constantly fell, injuring myself far more than the average baby typically does. My grandmother constantly urged my parents to get my health checked out by medical professionals because she knew something was medically wrong with me. My parents brought me to many different medical professionals, trying to figure out what was affecting my health. One surgeon wanted to give me an ear operation because they thought I had an acute inner ear imbalance. My parents brought me to a physiotherapist who assessed my motor skills. Based on their assessment, they said I might have Duchenne muscular dystrophy and recommended getting my doctor to test for it.

My doctor ordered a Kinase Creatine Level blood test, which indicated extreme elevations. This confirmed the diagnosis of Duchenne muscular dystrophy when I was two and a half years old. Duchenne muscular dystrophy (DMD) is an inherited genetic disorder primarily occurring in boys. People with DMD do not make a muscle protein called dystrophin, which causes all the muscles in the body to deteriorate, with 20-30% having intellectual and learning disabilities and early death. The medical research in 1996 said I would likely die by my nineteenth birthday.

This news devastated my family, especially my parents. In one moment, most of their aspirations and dreams for my future evaporated. I can only imagine how angry and helpless my parents felt, being unable to protect me from my illness. My parents separated when I was three years old. My two brothers and spent a few days of the week at my father's and some at my mother's.

As time went on, as a child, I became increasingly more emotionally withdrawn, angry, anxious, depressed, and resentful at life. I convinced myself that I was a huge burden to my family, believing it was my fault for making them stressed and sad. Often, young children with illnesses blame themselves for their family's distress, not understand that the illness was the culprit, not them. I told myself nobody loved me, wanted, or cared about me, and I felt I did not deserve to be loved. Often, when I was at my father's house, I would start crying, telling my father nobody loved me. My father tried to convince me that my family loved me, but I would deny his words, accusing him of lying to me. My not fully developed mind did not realize that my parents did love me, did the best they could do for me, and tried to provide me with the best medical treatments available.

When I was in elementary school, I was bullied, made fun of, insulted, punched, kicked, and pushed onto concrete because I was different and physically weaker than other students. I did not tell my parents I was bullied at school because I did not want to make them feel additional stress. I was so terrified of this bullying, that I often told my mom I did not want to go to school, and when I was being dropped off at school, I held onto the door frame of the car so hard that my parents would have to pull me out.

When I was eight years old, while at an appointment at the BC Children's Hospital Neuromuscular Clinic, the pediatric neurologist informed me in an insensitive and inappropriate manner that I was going to die at nineteen years of age from heart failure, or from pneumonia, or from choking on water or food. I knew what the neurologist told me was not right because of the cruel way he told me. It was scary and traumatizing. My mother wrote letters to the pediatric neurologist, saying how inappropriate this was. My mother always fought for me whenever others did not treat me fairly or respectfully. My mother always said that a mama bear will protect her children.

When I was ten years old, my father suspected I had dyslexia, a learning disability that causes difficulty or the inability to read, write, or spell. My dad encouraged me, saying, "You *are* going to learn how to read." He brought me to the reading specialist at my elementary school to show them I had dyslexia, and they confirmed that my father was right. After a year of intensive reading therapy, I could finally read. My dad always encouraged me when I wanted to quit reading therapy. I thank God for using my father to help me be able to read and excel academically. I was incredibly blessed by the father God gave me.

Also, at ten years old, my condition progressed to the point where my muscles were too weak for me to walk, and I needed to use a wheelchair. When I started using a wheelchair, my life drastically changed for the worse. I lost a lot of my personal freedom. I lost all my friends except for two. Those who abandoned me said things like, "I do not want to be friends with somebody in a wheelchair." With the two friends I still had, I could no longer hang out with them at their house after school due to wheelchair accessibility.

When I started using my wheelchair, the bullying further intensified, and people would call me a monster and tell me that nobody liked me or to go away. Due to being badly treated by other students, I developed significant social anxiety. When I was in middle school, most students ignored me and never talked to me. My classmates did not pick me for group assignments and generally excluded me. When I was in high school, the verbal insults directed toward me by other students were extremely damaging. My classmates would say cruel things to me like, "You will never graduate; you are not smart enough. " "Nobody likes you," and "Nobody's going to marry you or love you." I believed all the insults that my high school classmates told me and believed that nobody loved me or liked me and that I was a burden to everyone.

In high school, I felt intense isolation, rage, anger, and sadness that developed into extreme anxiety, depression, panic attacks, and intense thoughts of suicide. I had a well-thought-out plan for how to end my life! At age sixteen, I was in so much emotional and psychological pain, I felt that the only way to end the suffering was to die. At least then I would not be a burden to anybody anymore. After all, I would die early anyway, so why would it matter? This was the darkest place in my life, and I was going to end my life to escape the pain. Fortunately, God had other plans for me, and suicide was not His will for my life. God had a different story for me, one of victory, not of tragedy.

Chapter 2

GOD'S GIFT

*Th*ere are some people who we are destined to meet that will change our lives and make us who we are today. The people we cherish are gifts from Heaven that enrich our lives through their relationship with us. It is a blessing to have someone who treasures you, supports, believes in you, and encourages you to do your best.

When I was fourteen years old, God sent Jeanilyn, a Christian from the Philippines, to be employed by my father to take care of me at my father's house since he could no longer do so. Jeanilyn means "gift from God" or "the Lord is gracious." I believe God gave her the perfect name because she is a precious gift from God in my life, and God used her so that I would accept His gift of hope and salvation,

When I first met my caregiver, Jeanilyn, at my father's house, I tried everything to push her away. In fact, I did unpleasant things to her because I thought she would hurt me as other people had. I did not deserve to be loved, so I built a wall around my heart to protect myself. Pushing her away did not work. No matter how badly I treated her, she kept showing me God's grace and love through our relationship. Jeanilyn would cry out to God in prayer that I would change and accept Jesus as my Lord and personal Saviour, which was eventually effective. "The earnest prayer of a righteous person has great power and produces wonderful results" (James 5:16b, NLT). Over time, God used Jeanilyn to break the iron wall around my heart. If Jeanilyn had not prayed for me, I would not be alive today.

At sixteen, the cardiologist told me that the back wall of my heart looked thin and might eventually turn into a life-threatening hole. This was devastating news for me, and I was scared I would die at a young age. The pediatric orthopedic surgeon at the Children's Hospital said I needed heel cord surgery to straighten my feet and a spinal fusion surgery for my scoliosis by putting long metal rods around my spine to straighten it. The spinal fusion surgery would have significantly restricted my movements. I refused to get the surgeries done, because I saw how they affected somebody else with my illness, leaving them even more disabled. I felt extremely anxious, depressed, isolated, and terrified that I might die before nineteen years old. Because of my great despair, all I could think about was wanting to commit suicide at sixteen, but suicide was not God's plan for my life.

Jeanilyn kept persistently showing me God's love through her actions and kept encouraging me to go to church with her. I used to mock her faith in God and make fun of her for going to church, which did not stop her from inviting me to church and showing me God's love. She would cry out to God, praying for my salvation, and God answered by changing my personality.

Due to Jeanilyn's prayers for me, God divinely intervened by planting a thought in my head: "Before I kill myself, I want to see if God exists." It is a good thing God is real and living or I would not be alive. "Then you will call on me and come and pray to me, and I will listen to you" (Jeremiah 29:12, NIV). This was the major turning point in my life where God gave me a new story.

Chapter 3

A NEW CREATION

*S*ome of us come to a point where we are unhappy with ourselves and where life's direction is taking us. It seems like nothing is going right, and we do not know what to do. Then we feel sorry for ourselves and start wishing we could have had a different life. The good news is that there is hope because Jesus can transform our lives if we are willing to have a relationship with Him.

Jeanilyn's prayers for my salvation started showing results. I started to go to church every Sunday with Jeanilyn to her Pentecostal church, called Jesus Is Lord. Going to church was the first time I felt loved, because I could feel the love of God. After going to church with Jeanilyn for a couple of months, the worship team sang a song on one Sunday, called "Complete," sung by Parachute Band. Parts of the song went like: "So I lift my eyes to you, Lord. In your strength will I break through you, Lord. Touch me now. Let your love fall down on me. I know your love dispels all my fears. Through the storm, I will hold on, Lord. And by faith, I will walk on Lord… and I will be complete in you" (Parachute Band. Complete, 2001).

After singing those lyrics, I immediately felt the fire of the Holy Spirit touch me with extreme heat and an intense urgency to accept Jesus into my heart, and I accepted Jesus as my Lord and personal

Saviour. Immediately, after accepting Jesus, my whole life changed immediately. God freed me from the darkness, from my chains of anxiety, from depression, and from thoughts of suicide, and I found true peace that only God can give.

I knew then that my life was worth living, and I was a blessing. I was a new creation in Christ Jesus. The old Ryan was gone, and a new one had come. "Therefore, if anyone is in Christ, the new creation has come: The old has gone, the new is here!" (2 Corinthians 5:17, NIV). I felt whole and, over time, became calmer and joyful. I started to trust others, was kinder to others, and knew I was loved by my family and by Jeanilyn. I started trusting Jeanilyn, and our relationship developed into something like a mother-child relationship, and I became part of her Filipino family.

Six months after accepting Jesus as my Lord and Saviour, I experienced a miracle. When I went back to the cardiologist and got another heart ultrasound, they said the back wall of my heart looked healthy! It is medically impossible for the heart muscle to heal itself from the thinning of one of its walls, but through God, He made it possible. "Jesus looked at them and said, 'With man this is impossible, but with God all things are possible'" (Matthew 19:26, NIV).

In the winter of 2012, my steroid medication for Duchenne muscular dystrophy caused spinal compression fractures from osteoporosis. In other words, 50% of my vertebrae were fractured. It was one of the most painful experiences I ever went through. In six months, I experienced another miracle: my spinal pain disappeared! I got a back X-ray to see if my scoliosis had progressed, but the doctors were not expecting to see healed compression fractures in my spine. The doctors noticed that my spine healed in a way that caused it to be straighter, improving my scoliosis. Scoliosis surgery was no longer necessary! If I had gotten the scoliosis surgery, I likely would have died because the doctors and the orthopedic surgeon did not know I had severe osteoporosis. They didn't know because they couldn't take a bone density scan due to significant back pain. Doing the surgery would likely have caused crumpling of my spine, severe fractures, paralysis, and a high possibility of death. "Heal me, O Lord, and I will be healed; save me and I will be saved, for you are the one I praise" (Jeremiah 17:14, NIV).

When I accepted a personal relationship with Jesus, God performed miracles in my life and healed me emotionally, but He also healed my mind cognitively and intellectually. I used to struggle at school academically, and it was very difficult for me to achieve a C+ average, among other cognitive difficulties. When I met Jesus, He renewed my mind. I went from a C+ average to an A average. "And have put on the new self, which is being renewed in knowledge in the image of its Creator" (Colossians 3:10, NIV). Praise the Lord that I graduated high school with honours with distinction. When it was my turn to go across the stage during the graduation ceremony, I got a standing ovation from everyone in the audience and from the students graduating—even from those who told me I would never graduate. I was only able to achieve this with the help of God. "For with God nothing will be impossible" (Luke 1:37, NKJV). God is faithful, and He never left me during my difficulties.

If you want God to transform your life, heal you, and witness miracles like those He has done in my life, then wholeheartedly receive Jesus' gift of salvation by letting Him come into your heart and truly accept Him as your Lord and personal Saviour. Jesus is saying to you, "Here I am! I stand at the door and knock. If anyone hears my voice and opens the door, I will come in and eat with that person, and they with me" (Revelation 3:20, NIV). Jesus is kindly asking you if you want to have a personal relationship with Him by opening the door of your heart and letting Him in. Life with Jesus is beautiful, hopeful, purposeful, and worth living.

Accepting Jesus as your Lord and personal Saviour is the best decision you can make in your life. When you accept a personal relationship with Jesus, "He saved us, not because of the righteous things we had done, but because of his mercy. He washed away our sins, giving us a new birth and new life through the Holy Spirit" (Titus 3:5, NLT).

Chapter 4

SERVING GOD

*S*erving God gives us joy beyond human understanding as well as purpose, meaning, and direction. Being an obedient servant of God will cause us to step out of our comfort zone, mature spiritually, and place our trust in the Lord. Serving God is a blessing and a privilege and is something we can all do with the unique gifts the Lord has given us. "Shout for joy to the Lord, all the earth. Worship the Lord with gladness; come before him with joyful songs" (Psalm 100:1-2, NIV).

When I was seventeen and regularly attended JIL church services, the music ministry leader kept asking me for a year to join the music team as a backup singer. I kept saying no. I was shy at that time and still had social anxiety. After a year of saying no, the conviction of the Holy Spirit became so strong that I could no longer say no to God. At eighteen, I finally joined the music team and never regretted it. My eventual obedience to serve God in the music ministry gave me joy and purpose, helped me mature as a Christian, and helped me heal from my social anxiety. Deciding to serve God is amazing and fills your life with joy and blessings. When we obediently serve God, He can use us to bless other people's lives and lead people to a closer relationship with Jesus.

1 Peter 4:10-11, NLT – *God has given each of you a gift from his great variety of spiritual gifts. Use them well to serve one another. Do you have the gift of speaking? Then speak as though God himself were speaking through you. Do you have the gift of helping others? Do it with all the strength and energy that God supplies. Then everything you do will bring glory to God through Jesus Christ. All glory and power to him forever and ever! Amen.*

After a while, I started attending a weekly Bible study and a Night of Power meeting (a prayer meeting), which helped me further develop my faith and maturity as a Christian and my relationship with Jesus. After attending Bible study and Night of Power consistently, I was assigned to be the exhorter and prayer leader in which I opened and closed in prayer multiple times a month for church gatherings. While obeying God's assignments for me at church gatherings, He developed my gifts of preaching God's Word and public speaking. God gave me these gifts so that I might encourage others. Eventually, I became the manpower coordinator for Night of Power and for Sunday services. I knew becoming the manpower coordinator would be challenging, but I chose to obey God and rely on His strength because God rewards His faithful servants. Some days, serving God can be challenging, but it is still worth it.

Chapter 5

THE LORD BLESSES

There are seasons in our lives when we feel we are on top of the mountains, where everything is going right in life, and we have the prosperity of health, mind, and spirit. Praise God that He states to His children, "'For I know the plans I have for you,' declares the Lord, 'plans to prosper you and not to harm you, plans to give you hope and a future'" (Jeremiah 29:11, NIV).

In May of 2012, I turned nineteen years old and was significantly healthier than the doctors expected me to be for my age compared to other people with Duchenne muscular dystrophy. Many people with my illness died before they turned nineteen. But for me, the pediatric neurologist's prediction I would die at nineteen was proven incorrect, and I was still full of life. When we receive negative doctor reports, trust in Jesus! Our Great Physician can turn a tragedy report into a victory report. "Trust in the Lord with all your heart and lean not on your own understanding" (Proverbs 3:5, NIV).

In June of 2012, I started receiving government funding from a program allowing me to hire, pay my caregivers, and become more independent. With my new independence, I moved to my dad's house full-time for two months and then into my mom's basement suite with Jeanilyn and her family.

Despite having Duchenne muscular dystrophy, I pursued postsecondary education with the support of God, my family, and my Filipino family. I dreamed of becoming a registered clinical counsellor by getting my Bachelor of Arts in psychology, Master of Counselling degrees and receiving my registered clinical counsellor designation. When I told some individuals that I intended to pursue my Bachelor of Arts degree, they would say things like, "You do not have to do that; just enjoy your life." As a person with a physical disability, I was the target of societal stereotypes that people with physical disabilities do not belong in postsecondary school, that they are mentally incompetent, and are unable to achieve academic success. I did not let discouragement from people, institutions, and societal stereotypes prevent me from attending postsecondary school. When people discourage me from pursuing my dreams, I try even harder to accomplish my dreams. When I have a goal in mind, nothing can stop me from pursuing it with determination. I think I got my persistent personality trait from my mother.

In September of 2013, I started attending a local college to do the first half of my Bachelor of Arts in psychology degree. Initially, it was a little bit of a struggle setting up my accommodations and government funding with the college's Disability Resource Centre. Once I was provided with the computer software to help me read and write, my dyslexia was no longer a stumbling block to achieving academic excellence in postsecondary education. Also, I had a tutor who helped me write my paper assignments and encouraged me to do my best.

If it is God's will for you to achieve a specific dream or goal, He will make it happen regardless of the obstacles if you trust Him. I achieved higher academic excellence than I did in high school. For my bachelor's degree, I achieved a 90% average! Glory to God. "Commit your actions to the Lord, and your plans will succeed" (Proverbs 16:3, NLT). When you put your trust in the Lord, nothing is impossible if it is God's will. God did not allow my dyslexia or illness to prevent me from succeeding in postsecondary education because He prospers His children according to His will.

On March 16, 2013, my caregiver, Jeanilyn, gave birth to her first child, a baby boy named Joshua (EJ). I was excited when Joshua was born, because it was the first time I became an uncle. In Filipino culture, if you have a close relationship with the parent(s), you get to be an uncle or aunt of their child. I love being an uncle; it is a gift from God. I will never forget Joshua sitting on my lap while I drove my wheelchair around the house, making him laugh with excitement. Joshua looked up to me and asked me questions about interesting, weird, or serious topics. It is a wonderful feeling to be important in somebody else's life. Being an uncle to a child can fill you with so much joy, and it is amazing to see their accomplishments and see them learn and grow as a person. "Children are a gift from the Lord; they are a reward from him" (Psalm 127:3, NLT).

In May of 2013, Jeanilyn and her husband bought a house together. They were very excited that their prayers had come true to get a house in Canada. My dad and his two friends built a wooden ramp for me to be able to move into Jeanilyn's home with her family. They completed the ramp in time for me to celebrate my 20th birthday in Jeanilyn's home. I am so blessed to have a father who would drop everything to help me be happy and successful. My father wanted me to live in Jeanilyn's home because he knew I would be lonely and sad if I did not.

Starting in 2013, I started doing day trips to another city to attend JIL Church youth events that had invited youth from across the province of British Columbia. I could feel the love of Jesus in the atmosphere there, and the presence of God was so strong you could feel Him physically embrace you. Every time I attended those events, people would welcome me, talk to me with love in their hearts, and were excited to see me. It felt like I had a second home with other believers who love me with God's love. I could feel the unconditional love of God through the lives of those youths attending and running the youth events. I will never forget how amazed I was to see the power of God setting people free from the Devil and in seeing lives transforming right in front of my eyes. "Now the Lord is the Spirit, and where the Spirit of the Lord is, there is freedom" (2 Corinthians 3:17, NIV). Hearing people's testimonies, how God was working in their lives, and seeing their love and passion for serving God and others at the youth events inspired me, which helped me mature as a Christian and grow in my relationship with Jesus.

It is important for Christians to surround themselves with other believers to help them grow in their faith and encourage them during difficult times in life. Surrounding ourselves with other Christians who care about our well-being will help us strengthen our faith in God and mature us as Christians. "As iron sharpens iron, so one person sharpens another." (Proverbs 27:17, NIV).

In May of 2016, I started attending a local university to start the second half of my Bachelor of Arts in psychology degree. The first month of starting university was challenging, but I still did very well in my first term. To God be the glory, I was still achieving academic excellence with a 90% average. "For the Lord grants wisdom! From his mouth come knowledge and understanding" (Proverbs 2:6, NLT). If you have a personal relationship with Jesus and ask God to give you wisdom and understanding, He will give it to you.

On September 1, 2018, Jeanilyn gave birth to her second child, a baby girl named Janella. It was exciting having a niece for the first time in my life. Janella was loving, kind and bossy like her mother. She said good morning and good night and asked how I was doing. When Jeanilyn was taking care of me in the morning, Janella liked to help take care of me by cleaning my room with a duster, feeding me my breakfast, and giving me my pills. Janella wants to be a doctor or caregiver when she's older to take care of me. Jeanilyn's children are a gift and fill my life with happiness and joy; my life would not be the same without them. "Every good and perfect gift is from above, coming down from the Father of the heavenly lights, who does not change like shifting shadows" (James 1:17, NIV).

Chapter 6

THE LORD IS FAITHFUL

In life, there are seasons that are scary and confusing, and we do not know what to do. You doubt God's plan for your life and ask many questions. Sometimes, we find ourselves in a position where we ask God, "Why me? Why do I need to suffer?" God lets us go through those difficult seasons to build character, mature our faith, and gain a deeper trust in Him. Pain is an excellent teacher. During times of pain, we grow and learn the most.

> **Romans 5:3-5, NLT** – *We can rejoice, too, when we run into problems and trials, for we know that they help us develop endurance. And endurance develops strength of character, and character strengthens our confident hope of salvation. And this hope will not lead to disappointment. For we know how dearly God loves us, because he has given us the Holy Spirit to fill our hearts with his love.*

Sometimes, we do not understand God's plan for our lives, but His plan is always better than our plans. There is always a good reason why God lets us go through difficult seasons in our lives.

In November of 2018, every night, I would wake up at least eight times being out of breath, with heart racing, confused, and feeling like I was dying. I also had daytime sleepiness and headaches. When I went to my respirologist appointment that month, I told them about my symptoms, and they ordered an urgent arterial blood gas test to check my oxygen and carbon dioxide levels. They suspected I was not breathing properly due to sleep apnea (difficulty breathing when sleeping) or hypoventilation (breathing shallowly or slowly).

The test involved a large needle to puncture my artery deep inside my wrist. The pain of the puncture caused me to faint! The inside of our wrists have many sensitive nerves, making getting that test quite painful. When my respirologist saw the blood test results, they called me and told me that my carbon dioxide levels were extremely high. I had carbon dioxide poisoning. They told me that my carbon dioxide levels could cause me to slip into a coma or kill me while sleeping. My illness progressed to the point that I could not properly breathe while sleeping.

The respirologist organized with the hospital for me to be admitted to the respiratory ward as soon as a bed was available. The respiratory ward was so full that I had to wait three days before the hospital called to admit me. That was a scary three day wait. My life was in danger every time I slept until I got admitted to the hospital. I spent one week in the hospital using the hospital's BiPAP, a machine with an air hose attached to a mask that assists with breathing that I used while sleeping. Once I got my own BiPAP machine from a provincial respiratory equipment charity, I could go home.

It took me two months to get used to using my BiPAP machine while sleeping. I thank the Lord for protecting me from dying from carbon dioxide poisoning and providing me with a respirologist who advocated for me and looked out for my best interests. I got scared when I had carbon dioxide poisoning because I forgot to trust God and His promise never to leave me or to forsake me. Praise God that He does not abandon us in moments when we have disbelief or forget to trust Him. God reminded me to "Trust in the Lord with all your heart and lean not on your own understanding" (Proverbs 3:5-6, NIV). When we forget to trust in the Lord's promises and when we hear scary medical reports, we are filled with fear and focus on our feelings instead of praying to God for deliverance. God is greater than any negative medical report we can receive, because Jesus Has the power to conquer any sickness and disease.

In March of 2019, my left leg started to painfully swell with redness from the middle of my thigh to my feet. My leg was not infected, and I ignored it, thinking it was a leg muscle injury I was unaware of because Duchenne muscular dystrophy means muscles are prone to injury. After two weeks of my leg swelling, the pain became too painful to tolerate, so I went to the Emergency Department.

The emergency doctor I saw discriminated against me due to my illness and disability because of the common stereotype in the medical field that people with disabilities are "mentally incompetent." The doctor treated me like I was unintelligent and did not believe me about my symptoms. He lied and told me it was an infection and tried to prescribe antibiotics. I knew I was being lied to because I had had leg infections in the past. I did not have a skin rash, and the doctor did not tell me the blood test results. When the doctor was trying to write a prescription for antibiotics, the Holy Spirit gave me the strength to yell at the doctor, "Something is wrong with me, and you need to fix it!" I was shocked I was given the strength to yell at the doctor.

The doctor still did not believe me about my symptoms and told me to come back to the Emergency Department the next day and get a leg ultrasound. He clearly wanted to get rid of me. I returned the next day to the Emergency Department and told the check-in nurse that the doctor from the day before had told me to come back to get a leg ultrasound.

Fortunately, when I saw the emergency doctor who was on shift that day, he was kind, understanding, and believed me about my leg symptoms. He ordered an ultrasound of my leg because the previous doctor had not ordered one. After my leg ultrasound, the ultrasound technician told me to return to the Emergency Department as soon as possible because I had a large blood clot in my left thigh.

I knew blood clots were serious, but I did not know how serious it was until the doctor told me. When I saw the doctor again, he told me the ultrasound indicated I had a huge blood clot in my left thigh, a result of all the medications I was taking. Then the doctor got angry and said, "The doctor you saw yesterday could have killed you because he made you wait for an ultrasound. If part of the blood clot in your thigh broke off, you could have died if it travelled to your brain or lungs. It could have killed you!" I could tell the doctor was furious with the other doctor I had seen the previous day.

The new doctor gave me two heparin injections in my stomach, which is medication to dissolve blood clots quickly. The heparin injections feel like a bee sting, lasting for a few minutes. After receiving my two injections, I was given a bottle of blood thinner tablets to take home to dissolve the blood clot and a prescription for more blood thinners. I was told I could go home.

When I was leaving the Emergency Department, I saw the new doctor confront the doctor from the day before. He yelled at him, saying he could have killed his patient! It filled me with joy because God served justice on my behalf by punishing the doctor who discriminated against me. "When justice is done, it brings joy to the righteous but terror to evildoers" (Proverbs 21:15, NIV). Since God is just, He will punish people who do evil, especially those who do evil toward those who have a personal relationship with Jesus. God's "Righteousness and justice are the foundation of your throne; love and faithfulness go before you" (Proverbs 89:14, NIV). I praise the Lord for protecting me from people who do evil to me. "But the Lord is faithful, and he will strengthen you and protect you from the evil one" (2 Thessalonians 3:3, NIV). If you would like to experience the faithfulness of God, His strength and protection from evil requires that you genuinely accept Jesus as your Lord and personal Saviour with all your heart.

In December of 2019, I started experiencing difficulty breathing, shortness of breath, and dizziness, so I went to the hospital's Emergency Department to determine the issue. The emergency doctor told me my blood test results were fine. My carbon dioxide levels were slightly high, and my oxygen levels were slightly low, but it was nothing to be concerned about. I was still experiencing breathing difficulties, so I mentioned to the doctor that I had a portable mouthpiece ventilator at home that I was not using.

A mouthpiece ventilator is a machine with an air hose connected to a mouthpiece that looks like a straw in front of your mouth that you puff on every five to ten seconds to get pressurized air into your lungs. This forces you to have deeper breaths. The emergency doctor recommended I start using my mouthpiece ventilator because my illness was affecting the muscles that helped me breathe. Six months earlier, my respirologist recommended I start using a mouthpiece ventilator. I stubbornly did not listen to their advice, because I refused to accept that my illness would progressively affect my breathing.

When I got home from the hospital, I started using the mouthpiece ventilator and my breathing problems and dizziness significantly improved. It was challenging to accept being completely reliant on my BiPAP and mouthpiece ventilator for me to breathe. Through this experience, God taught me that relying on medical science is not a lack of faith, because God gave doctors wisdom to help people live longer. "On hearing this, Jesus said, 'It is not the healthy who need a doctor, but the sick'" (Matthew 9:12, NIV). Jesus tells us that we should go to a doctor if we are sick or have an illness. If a doctor prescribes medication for a health condition and the patient refuses to take the medication and prays for healing and dies as a result, that is not faith but a lack of wisdom.

Chapter 7

THE GOD OF VICTORY

In life, we must go through seasons of great difficulty before we can get to seasons of great victory. Getting to your victory takes hard work, trials, and testing. If you are unwilling to do the hard work and endure difficult times, you will not succeed. Do not give up on your dreams and goals when it gets difficult or when somebody discourages you—they are learning opportunities for you to grow. The Lord tells us, "You will eat the fruit of your labor; blessings and prosperity will be yours" (Psalm 128:2, NIV). Hard work makes victories taste sweet.

There were times in my life when I wanted to give up, but I chose to work hard at achieving my goals regardless of how I felt, because I knew the end goal would be rewarding. I would rather struggle to achieve my goals and dreams than quit and give up. The Lord gave me a spirit of courage and persistence to face difficult situations and to achieve the goals and dreams in my life that are in His will. God says, "But as for you, be strong and do not give up, for your work will be rewarded" (2 Chronicles 15:7, NIV).

To God be the glory in June of 2019, I graduated with my Bachelor of Arts in psychology with a 90% average at my local university with the support of God, my family, and my Filipino family. I worked hard for six years to get my Bachelor of Arts degree, so it felt very rewarding to roll my wheels across the stage again and receive my diploma.

The joy of getting my Bachelor of Arts degree wore off after a few days, and I started working on the next milestone in my academic journey. I told people I wanted to get my master's degree in counselling. The majority of the people I told about this gave a positive response with encouraging words. A few people gave negative responses, such as, "Getting your bachelor's degree is good enough! Getting a master's degree will be too difficult." Such responses showed their doubts in my abilities or that they felt envy, making them unhappy to see me achieve my goals.

When I receive negative responses to my successes, I keep shut my mouth and continue working hard at my goals and dreams, because I know words cannot stop me. When we have successes in our lives, there will always be people who will try to discourage us, doubt us, and are not happy with our successes. The best way to handle this is to concentrate on the encouraging words from the people who believe you can achieve your goals. Do not let other people's discouraging words prevent you from achieving your goals and dreams.

When I started my bachelor's degree, I knew that there were very few jobs available for people with a Bachelor of Arts in psychology. I needed a master's degree in counselling to get a job. A few months before getting my diploma, I applied for the Master of Arts in Counselling Psychology program at my local University. A few weeks after my graduation, the university told me I was not accepted into the program because the other applications were more ambitious and had more volunteer experience and better references. I was disappointed that the university did not even interview me and judged me based on my resume only.

Since I was not accepted into the counselling program at the local university, I wondered if it was God's plan for me to get my counselling degree at all. A few months before I applied for the counselling program at the local university, my mother gave me a newspaper article about another counselling program in another city thirty minutes away from where I lived. So, I applied to the counselling program in the article my mother gave me. I was discouraged about being rejected from my first application. In June of 2019, I applied for the Master of Counselling program at the second university.

At the end of June, I received an email from a school official to set up an interview with the counselling program's director. The entrance interview was set up at the end of June 2019, which I must pass to get accepted into the program. I was nervous about the interview. This was my last chance to get into a counselling program, because moving to another city to go to school was not possible for me. Two JIL Church members, who were my temporary caregivers, and their husbands filling in for my other caregivers, brought me to the interview. When we were outside of the building, I told them I was nervous. They suggested we pray, so we prayed together for the victory to pass the interview. It was a very difficult entrance interview with the director. At the beginning of the interview, the director made a statement I needed to challenge. The statement was: "I do not think you are old enough or have enough life experience to get accepted into the program. Prove me wrong." And then I was asked questions like, "Why do you deserve to be accepted into the program? What is your future plan if you get a Master of Counselling degree? What counselling perspectives would you use with clients?"

When I opened my mouth, the Holy Spirit spoke for me. I was astonished that the Holy Spirit gave me the ability to answer the interview questions with amazing answers. After the interview, the director said he was amazed at how I answered his questions. He told me he had never heard somebody answer the interview questions like that before. He told me I had passed the entrance interview, and I had a spot in the Master of Counselling program. "But thanks be to God! He gives us the victory through our Lord Jesus Christ" (1 Corinthians 15:57, NIV). From this experience, the Lord taught me that if He has a plan for me, He will carry it out to completion. "Being confident of this, that He who began a good work in you will carry it on to completion until the day of Christ Jesus" (Philippians 1:6, NIV).

The few months before I started the Master of Counselling program, I had difficulties setting up my disability accommodations with the new university. It was frustrating because, without my accommodation sctup, I would not be able to start the Master of Counselling program. The university did not properly train their disability advisor and administration staff on how to accommodate students with disabilities and how to get government funding for students with disabilities. The Lord encouraged me not to give up and to continue pursuing my dream of becoming a mental health counsellor. So, instead of giving up, I taught the disability advisor and administration staff how to get disability funding and accommodations for students with disabilities. Due to being persistent, I was able to start the Master of Counselling program at the expected start date of the program. "For I can do everything through Christ who gives me strength" (Philippians 4:13, NLT).

In October of 2019, I started the Master of Counselling program. The program was structured extremely different than my Bachelor of Arts program. There were no exams or tests except one comprehensive exam, numerous online discussion posts, and many writing assignments. It was very fast-paced and a 73% was a failing grade. Since the Master of Counselling program was skill-based, unlike my bachelor's degree, I could not rely on memorization to do well. The Master of Counselling program is graded on your ability to write at a graduate level, acquire counselling skills, self-knowledge, self-reflection, and self-growth. But by God's glory, I was achieving a 92% average. If you lack wisdom and knowledge, ask God, "For the Lord grants wisdom! From his mouth come knowledge and understanding" (Proverbs 2:6, NLT).

Chapter 8

THROUGH THE VALLEY OF DEATH

*S*ometimes, there are seasons in our lives where we are overwhelmed with fear, pain, and grief due to the death of a loved one, experiencing the trauma of a personal near-death medical event, or from receiving a devastating diagnosis of a health condition. Those are some of the most terrifying experiences we can endure, because they remind us that death cannot be controlled or reversed, can happen at any moment, and that each of us will all die one day. Praise God: "Even though I walk through the darkest valley, I will fear no evil, for you are with me; your rod and your staff, they comfort me" (Psalm 23:4, NIV).

In January of 2020, my Duchenne muscular dystrophy progressed to the point that singing as a backup singer at the church was no longer safe for me. Singing prevented me from getting enough oxygen, causing dizziness and lightheaded. Fainting would be dangerous because my multipiece ventilator does not work when I am unconscious…and I could die from a lack of oxygen.

In fact, one day, I was singing as a backup singer for the Sunday service, and at the last song of the service, I started to feel dizzy, having blurred tunnel vision, and everything seemed dark. After the service was over, I told the leader of music ministry that I could no longer sing as a backup singer due to my compromised breathing.

It was a significant loss for me that I could no longer sing to serve God and lead people into the presence of God through singing. I started grieving because I could no longer continue to enjoy a major aspect of my life that gave me purpose. However, I continued to serve God as the Manpower coordinator for the church.

Besides stepping down from the music team, everything else was still going well until the end of January 2020 when I got a cold virus that started with a sore throat and stuffy nose and turned into a chest cold. I was concerned it might become pneumonia but did not think much about it. Having compromised breathing due to my illness and being immunocompromised from using steroids as a treatment for my illness puts me at a significant risk of dying from pneumonia.

My chest cold continued to worsen because I could not cough out the phlegm in my lungs well enough, making breathing progressively harder. Eventually, it became a struggle to breathe. I felt dizzy, looked pale, and my heart was painful and beating very fast. I rushed to go to the hospital's Emergency Department on February 12, 2020. When it was my turn to see the emergency check-in nurse, I was experiencing intense heart pain. They checked my heart rate, oxygen saturation, and blood pressure. My heart rate was 170, and I had low oxygen saturation and high blood pressure. When the nurse saw this, they rushed me in to see the emergency doctor as soon as possible. I knew my life was in danger, especially if I did not receive medical treatment quickly.

Emergency doctors do not see you immediately unless your life is in danger. I eventually learned that an adult having heart pain with a resting heart rate of 170 could die if urgent treatment is not received. The doctor ordered an EKG for my heart, blood tests, and a chest X-ray. I was diagnosed with pneumonia in both lungs, given medication to treat my pneumonia, and admitted to the hospital's respiratory ward. Having pneumonia meant there was a high possibility of dying due to complications of my illness. Many people with Duchenne muscular dystrophy died from pneumonia, including a few I knew.

While I stayed at the hospital for six days, receiving my antibiotic pneumonia IV treatment, many things happened to me. I almost choked to death twice from phlegm being stuck in my throat. The nurses had to do an emergency deep throat suction to suck the phlegm out of my throat so I could breathe again. One night when I was sleeping, I woke up unable to breathe. I turned my head to the left side of the bed, and I saw the spiritual being known as the Angel of Death standing beside my bed, the same one in Exodus 12:23. The Angel of Death was nine feet tall, wearing an ash grey robe torn up at the hems with a hood hiding his face. I knew the Angel of Death had come to kill me, to take my soul from my body.

Then the Angel of Death said, "It is time for you to die."

But Jesus said, "Leave him alone; it is not his time yet."

The Angel of Death disappeared at Jesus's command, and I could breathe again. The next night, when I was sleeping, the Angel of Death visited again in my dream and said, "It is time for you to die."

But again, Jesus commanded, "Leave him alone; it is not his time yet."

Every time the Lord said that command to the Angel of Death, I could feel His authority, power, and love filling me with comfort and peace. The Lord Jesus Christ has authority over angels, demons, and death itself. "Our God is a God who saves! The Sovereign Lord rescues us from death" (Psalm 68:20, NLT). Thank the Lord that He protected me from dying from pneumonia. When my pneumonia infection cleared up, I was discharged from the hospital and went home.

On Tuesday, February 18, one day after being home from the hospital, I woke up in the morning feeling slightly nauseous and dizzy, so I thought I was just hungry and ignored it, going about my day. By the afternoon, I felt extremely dizzy, nauseous, and had difficulty breathing, and my face was pale white. I knew something was wrong, so I decided to go to the hospital's Emergency Department to get it checked out. As I was going to the hospital, I started gasping for air, and my face turned very pale because I could not breathe properly. Gasping for air is a terrifying experience because your body desperately tries to get more oxygen into the lungs while your mind tells you that you might die soon.

When I arrived at the Emergency Department, I saw the check-in nurse immediately. While gasping for air, I told the check-in nurse my symptoms with difficulty. They checked my oxygen saturation, and it was at 80%. Looking shocked and alarmed, they admitted me immediately to see the doctor. The nurse took action instantly because if blood oxygen saturation drops below 80%, you can get brain damage, organ damage, and death if not given immediate medical care.

As soon as I arrived at my emergency room, the nurse gave me oxygen, trying to prevent my oxygen from dropping further. The emergency doctor ordered an urgent chest X-ray to understand what was happening to me. While waiting for the X-ray, the nurses and doctors would check on me every five minutes to ensure I was still alive. As soon as the emergency doctor got the results, they told me that my right lung was 45% collapsed and was starting to push on my heart, which could cause my heart to stop beating. The doctor diagnosed me with a spontaneous pneumothorax, the sudden onset of a collapsed lung without apparent cause. It is usually caused when a small area of lung tissue is filled with air and then ruptures, causing the air to leak into the space around the lung, which collapses your lungs. It was suspected I got my spontaneous pneumothorax from coughing too hard when I had pneumonia.

The emergency doctor told me that the medical team was getting ready to preform an emergency procedure on me. They purposely did not tell me what the procedure was to prevent additional stress putting me over the edge and potentially killing me. Around 45 minutes later, a doctor came into my emergency room and asked me if I consented to them performing a chest tube procedure to re-expand my lung.

A chest tube procedure is when they inject you with a local anesthetic to numb the first two centimetres of skin and muscle, then puncture you with a large hollow needle to insert a flexible metal guidewire of about ten centimetres into the membrane around your lung. When the guidewire is in place, they make a one-inch-wide incision in the skin, slide a large pointed rod and chest tube on top of the guidewire, and then use a rod to force the chest tube ten centimetres into your lung membrane. When the chest tube is in place, they remove the guidewire and metal rod, leaving the chest tube inside of you and sew it securely to the skin. This procedure is typically done when you are awake and are given ketamine or hydromorphone before the procedure starts. Ketamine can produce awake sedation and is a potent pain reliever, while hydromorphone is a strong narcotic pain reliever. Chest tube procedures are the most painful medical procedure you can experience—more painful than giving birth and breaking multiple bones, even when given ketamine or hydromorphone.

They were right. The pain I experienced during the chest tube procedure was unimaginable. Chest tube procedures are painful because the local anesthetic only numbs the first two centimeters of skin and muscle, not inside the lung membrane. So, you can feel the sharp point of the metal guidewire, pointed rod, and the chest tube being inserted ten centimeters inside your lung membrane, scratching and scraping you. It felt like a scalpel cutting me from the inside. It was pure torture. It caused me to shout in pain for five minutes straight. The excruciating sensation was like bubble wrap exploding inside me, and I thought all my rib bones had broken—though they hadn't. I hoped I would never experience the horrific trauma of another chest tube procedure.

During the chest tube procedure, I forgot to use my mouthpiece ventilator due to the neurological effects of ketamine. After about seven minutes of not using my mouthpiece ventilator, I fell unconscious due to a lack of oxygen getting to my brain. The medical staff forgot to hook me up to the oxygen monitoring device, and they were so busy assisting with the chest tube procedure to realize I had fallen unconscious because of the lack of oxygen.

When I was unconscious for about two minutes, I went to Heaven. Heaven was bright, sunny, and warm, with blue skies and fluffy white clouds, and I could feel peace and joy, no more suffering, pain, or tears. God promises that if we are accepted into Heaven that "He will wipe every tear from their eyes, and there will be no more death or sorrow or crying or pain. All these things are gone forever" (Revelation 21:4, NLT). I was angry at God because He had brought me back to earth instead of letting me die so I could stay in Heaven. Being in Heaven is a paradise with unending joy and no suffering, and I was angry that I could not stay.

I regained consciousness shortly after the chest tube procedure was complete, and the doctor told me, "You have been admitted to the Intensive Care Unit (ICU), and your ICU room is ready for you." I was still in critical condition while waiting for the chest tube to re-expand my right lung. The last thing I remembered was going to my ICU room before the ketamine completely blocked out my memory for the next day.

The next thing I remember was sitting in my bed in the ICU as the Critical Care Doctor told me the X-ray showed that the chest tube was kinked inside me and another chest tube procedure was required. That terrified me. The first one was traumatic. I didn't want to go through another. The doctor explained that because the chest tube inside me was kinked, the air in the lung membrane could not escape to allow the lung to re-expand. The tube had become kinked when I was using my sling and the hospital's lift to transfer me into the ICU bed. The Critical Care Doctor told me I would get another sometime that day.

Later, a different doctor entered to tell me that she would do my second chest tube procedure. I was confused, because I was not assigned to be her patient, but this doctor proceeded to do the procedure anyway without getting permission from the Critical Care Doctor. This new doctor did not check the X-ray like she was supposed to, unaware that people with Duchenne muscular dystrophy have organ anatomy higher in the body than somebody without the illness. She then gave me an injection of ketamine, which was dangerous since I'd just had one two days before. Too much ketamine can be toxic and damaging to the body.

The second chest tube procedure was less painful because I was able to hold Jeanilyn during the procedure, but I still shouted in pain. Unfortunately, the metal guidewire and chest tube were not properly inserted, causing blood to go into the chest tube, indicating that the doctor had punctured an organ or a blood vessel. The doctor had to leave the chest tube inside the punctured organ to focus on preventing me from hemorrhaging blood.

In the end, it was a fiasco. The critical care doctor told me to stop taking my medications in case I needed emergency surgery due to the other doctor negligently performing the second chest tube procedure. A CT scan revealed that the chest tube had scratched my diaphragm and punctured my liver all the way through. The tube was still in my liver! That set off an explosion as the critical care doctor chewed out the doctor who had performed the chest tube procedure. The doctor had committed three significant medical malpractice offences.

The Devil tried to use the doctor who did the chest tube procedure as an instrument to try to kill me. Jesus said this of the Devil, "The thief comes only to steal and kill and destroy; I have come that they may have life, and have it to the full" (John 10:10, NIV). If the Holy Spirit had not intervened by guiding the chest tube away from my stomach, heart, or from a major blood vessel, I would have died! If the chest tube had been placed an inch in a different direction, I wouldn't have survived.

The doctors monitored my liver, worried that it would bleed if they removed the chest tube from it. The chest tube was left inside my liver for two days, causing me excruciating pain, which required high doses of intravenous hydromorphone. Being in significant pain and on high doses of hydromorphone caused me to have horrible nightmares. In the nightmares, all my loved ones were bloodily murdered with a knife. I often woke up with sweat all over my body and shouting in fear until I realized it was a dream.

It had been two days since the doctors had taken me off all my medications in case I needed surgery on the liver. This caused me to have an acute adrenal crisis due to being off my steroids for two days. This is caused by a lack of cortisol. My blood pressure dropped to 70/60, and my blood sugar dropped extremely low—a deadly combination. The medical team was unaware I was having an acute adrenal crisis, so I wasn't being correctly treated to regulate my blood pressure or blood sugar. The doctors, my family, my caregivers, and I thought I would die in a few days because no medical treatment was working, and my body was shutting down.

To make things even worse, I had two visitors come to my ICU room, and one of them said to me, "Stop fighting to live so you can pass away peacefully." The other visitor supported what the first had said. Telling somebody to give up and die are words from the Devil. I ignored them and chose to fight to survive, because I was too stubborn to die, and I was not done with life yet.

It was not God's plan for me to die in that situation. Instead, God performed miracles. The doctor removed the chest tube from my body and did another CT scan to see if I was bleeding inside. Somehow the puncture holes in my liver had closed by themselves! Boy did he have a confused look on his face! They could not understand how the puncture holes in my liver had healed themselves instantly after the chest tube had been removed. Technically, that was medically impossible. I did not require surgery anymore to fix my liver. God made the impossible possible with His power.

On the second day of having an acute adrenal crisis, the Holy Spirit gave me the wisdom to start taking my steroids again against the doctor's order. Within twelve hours of retaking my steroids, my blood pressure and blood sugar started normalizing to healthy levels.

Praise the Lord. God is so good to help me survived three life-and-death medical crises within four days. "Taste and see that the Lord is good; blessed is the one who takes refuge in him" (Psalm 34:8, NIV). You, too, can have this promise of God if you wholeheartedly accept Jesus and give your life to follow Him.

After a few days of stabilizing from coming out of an acute adrenal crisis, I was no longer in critical condition. I was discharged from the ICU and admitted to the Respiratory Ward. After being in the Respiratory Ward for a few days, everything seemed to be going well, and the medical staff thought I would be discharged in several more days since my lung had not re-collapsed. Everything seemed fine until I felt a sharp, painful pop sensation in my right lung.

The nurse said everything was okay, and they let the doctor know. After several hours, my throat felt tight, and I had difficulty breathing. The nurse checked my oxygen saturation, which was on the low side, so they informed the doctor immediately. Shortly after, I had an urgent chest X-ray to see if my right lung had re-collapsed. It had completely collapsed, putting me in critical condition again. An hour after the X-ray, the respirologist came into my hospital room and said we needed to do another chest tube procedure right away. Again, I was terrified. The last two experiences had been traumatic!

This was the third chest tube procedure, but they could not give me ketamine, only hydromorphone, making the procedure even more excruciatingly painful than the last two. I shouted even louder during that Chest tube procedure than the last two. I probably shouted so loud I could be heard in the hallways of the hospital. The respirologist and the nurse assisting in the procedure were surprised at how well I took the pain because I did not cry, move all over the place, or faint like most patients do. They told me that they had seen big, strong, macho men cry like a baby during chest tube procedures. Five minutes after receiving my hydromorphone injection, I fell asleep in relief of no longer being in severe pain. The Holy Spirit gave me the strength to endure the horrible pain of chest tube procedures.

"The Lord is my strength and my song; he has given me victory" (Psalm 118:14, NLT).

About a week later, they removed the third chest tube because my lung was fully re-expanded, but once again, my right lung collapsed, resulting in a fourth chest tube procedure. The doctors thought it would be a good idea to try something different because the previous three procedures had not worked to keep my lung inflated. About a week after having the fourth chest tube procedure, they sent me home with the chest tube still inside me with a one-way valve attached to the outside of my body. They would remove it in a month. They felt they needed to give the hole in my lung more time to heal. They hoped that would prevent a re-collapse of the lung.

A month later, I went to my hospital appointment and had the fourth chest tube removed. I had to wait at the hospital for two hours to get a chest X-ray, which is standard protocol. While waiting for the chest X-ray, I started experiencing right lung pain, but the X-ray showed nothing was wrong with my lung, and I was sent home.

After being home for a few days, I felt another sharp, painful popping sensation in my right lung, so I had to return to the hospital, be admitted to the ICU, and had yet a fifth chest tube procedure done. This time, the doctors came up with a new approach to prevent my lung from re-collapsing again. When my lung was fully re-expanded, they told me they would perform a pleurodesis to my right lung membrane. Pleurodesis is a thirty-minute medical procedure where they put medical talc powder or medication into your lung membrane to produce scar tissue that causes your lung to adhere to the lung lining, which would prevent recurrent collapsed lungs.

Before the respirologist did the pleurodesis procedure, they told me they would inject talc powder dissolved in water into my chest tube. They instructed me to move around for 30 minutes while taking deep breaths to spread the talc solution evenly as part of the procedure. They told me I would feel significantly uncomfortable due to a burning sensation, difficulty breathing, and pain for thirty minutes. They were right. It was significantly painful for thirty minutes but less painful than a chest tube procedure. After thirty minutes, the respirologist returned and drew out the talc solution with a syringe, which reduced the pain significantly.

About two weeks later, the respirologist removed the fifth chest tube, but after a few hours, I felt another sharp, painful pop sensation in my right lung again. The doctors ordered another chest X-ray that showed my right lung had partially collapsed, and the top part of my lung was sticking to the scar tissue of the lung membrane. The only good thing that the X-ray told the doctors was that the first pleurodesis procedure had been about 50% successful.

The respirologist had to perform a *sixth* chest tube procedure to re-expand my lower right lung, but this time, they used a smaller tube than the previous five. Around a week later, my right lung was fully re-expanded and the respirologist performed a second pleurodesis, injecting a much larger amount of talc solution than the previous pleurodesis, hoping it would scar my whole right lung lining. This pleurodesis was more painful due to the greater amount of talc solution used.

Around three weeks later, the respirologist removed the sixth chest tube, and I did *not* feel another sharp, painful pop sensation in my right lung this time. Since I had no symptoms of a collapsed lung, the doctors ordered another chest X-ray about 2½ weeks later to be safe. The X-ray showed no sign of a collapsed lung, but it did show thick scar tissue inside my entire right lung lining that my whole right lung had firmly attached to.

I asked my respirologist how likely it would be for my right lung to collapse again, and they told me less than a 5% chance. In fact, the only possible way for my lung to re-collapse was if I got stabbed in the lung or got in a severe car accident that broke my ribs. A few days later, the doctors finally released me from the hospital, and my right lung did not re-collapse. Praise the Lord! I was in and out of the hospital for 4½ months. I had pneumonia, six chest tube procedures, two pleurodeses, almost died ten times, saw the angel of death twice, and went to Heaven for a few minutes. That was a lot to experience in a 4½ month period, but because of the greatness and goodness of God, He performed medically impossible miracles and protected me from death.

About one out of five people with Duchenne muscular dystrophy die from pneumonia and have a 40% chance of death every time they have a collapsed lung. It is statistically impossible that I survived pneumonia and six collapsed lungs, but I survived because God is the God of impossibilities. The Holy Spirit gave me the power to endure many excruciatingly painful medical procedures. "But those who hope in the Lord will renew their strength. They will soar on wings like eagles; they will run and not grow weary, they will walk and not be faint" (Isaiah 40:31, NIV). After seeing God's incredible power in my life while I was at the hospital, there was no doubt in my mind that God was 100% real as a physical person.

Despite being in and out of the hospital and having near-death experiences over 4½ months, God gave me the strength, knowledge, and wisdom to continue to do my Master of Counselling program when I was extremely sick. God knew I was too persistent to stop my schooling, even in the face of death, so He made it so I could continue my studies.

As long as I am alive, I will live my life to the fullest, so when it is my time to go to Heaven, I will have no regrets. Death is the only thing that can stop me from pursuing my dreams and goals in life. When I die, I will receive the victory of eternal salvation with Jesus in Heaven.

Chapter 9

BROKEN IN SPIRIT

*S*ome of us will suffer horrible trauma(s), tragic loss(es), or the death of somebody significant in our lives that will break our hearts and minds. "The human spirit can endure in sickness, but a crushed spirit who can bear?" (Proverbs 18:14, NIV). Our trauma and grief can sometimes be unbearably painful, making life feel hopeless, even to the point where believing the lie that suicide is the only solution. Suicide is not God's plan for our lives, and suicide breaks God's heart and the hearts of people close to you.

After returning home from the hospital, my health remained stable, and I did exceptionally well in the Master of Counselling program. Physically and academically, everything was good, but psychologically, I was extremely broken from the medical trauma of having six chest tube procedures, two pleurodesis procedures, almost dying ten times, and experiencing discrimination and prejudice from the medical staff.

In addition, I was grieving because my respirologist told me that I could never go to church again in person and that I needed to avoid going inside buildings with people because if I got any cold or flu virus, there is a high probability I would get pneumonia and die. They told me that even if the COVID-19 pandemic ended, I would die if I chose to go to church in person and ended up with pneumonia again.

With this and with what I had experienced, I suffered from medical trauma, severe anxiety and panic attacks, constantly thinking I would die. The grief that I could never join in-person church fellowships, be in the church music team, and could no longer be the Manpower coordinator ever again overwhelmed me. I became angry with God because He did not allow me to die so I could go to Heaven. In truth, the real reason I was angry with God was because He allowed me to live to experience unbearable suffering from trauma, grief, and loss. I longed for Heaven, peace, joy, and no suffering, pain, or sorrow.

My mental health further deteriorated to the point where I was experiencing intense posttraumatic stress symptoms and constant thoughts of suicide. I started praying to God, "Please kill me; I do not want to suffer anymore. Let me die so I can go to Heaven and finally rest." No matter how much I begged God for death, He would say no. The only thing that comforted me during this painful part of life was listening to praise and worship music and reading the Bible. I spent hours listening to Christian praise and worship music—especially when I was extremely anxious. God often whispered to me during those times very clearly, "Do not worry, My son; everything is going to be okay."

Whenever God said this to me, I cried because of the intimate love of God, the Heavenly Father comforting me. "Praise be to the God and Father of our Lord Jesus Christ, the Father of compassion and the God of all comfort" (2 Corinthians 1:3, NIV). It took many months for me to believe God that everything would be all right. The Holy Spirit used a Christian song by Jeremy Camp, titled "The Story's Not Over," to keep me going. Some of the song lyrics that had a significant impact on me were: "I've been through so much through the years. I've had heartbreak, heartbreak. I kept reaching for You through the tears. The story's not over yet. You've got it under control" (Jeremy Camp. The Story's Not Over, 2019). The

Holy Spirit used those lyrics to let me know God saw all the suffering I had been through over the years; He still had a purpose for my life, and everything was under His control. "And we know that in all things God works for the good of those who love him, who have been called according to his purpose" (Romans 8:28, NIV).

After one or two months of experiencing posttraumatic stress and grief symptoms, I decided to get counselling from a clinical counsellor. I contacted about fifty counsellors, and all of them, except for two, said either they did not feel comfortable counselling a person with a physical disability or that they did not have the proper training to provide disability counselling. I was shocked to learn that there was significant discrimination toward persons with disabilities in the field of counselling, because counsellors are trained to be compassionate, empathetic, and ethical.

I chose one of the two counsellors who said they would work with me. The counsellor I chose specialized in trauma, posttraumatic stress, and anxiety. The counsellor seemed like a good match for me, and I started having weekly sessions for a few months. After counselling with them for two months, I revealed to them that I was a Christian, and they told me they were also a Christian. The counsellor kept encouraging me with Bible references, reminding me to pray and read my Bible. After four months of counselling, my symptoms of anxiety, panic attacks, posttraumatic stress, grief, and thoughts of suicide were almost completely gone. The Lord encourages us to seek wise counsel, such as a friend, a family member, or a counsellor. "Where there is no counsel, the people fall; But in the multitude of counselors there is safety" (Proverbs 11:14, NKJV). If you are significantly struggling with your mental health, seek clinical counselling. God is not against people receiving clinical counselling, and the Bible encourages us to seek out wise counsel, which produces wisdom.

After being out of the hospital for four months, I experienced a minor setback with difficulty breathing. Back at the hospital on October 29, 2020, I was diagnosed with bronchitis (infection of bronchial tubes in the lungs), which can turn into pneumonia. I also had a severe leg infection. I received IV antibiotic treatment for my bronchitis and leg infection. I was worried that all the coughing caused by the bronchitis would create a hole in my left lung and cause it to collapse. Since I had two pleurodesis procedures performed in my right lung lining, I knew that one, at least, could not collapse. My respirologist ordered a chest X-ray, which revealed that my lungs were fine, and there was no sign of any collapsed lung. Two weeks later, my bronchitis and leg infections cleared up, and I was discharged from the hospital. The hospital stay gave me moderate anxiety symptoms, which were gone after another month of counselling.

With the help of the Holy Spirit and counselling, I overcame anxiety, posttraumatic stress, and persistent thoughts of suicide. The year of 2020 was a long, challenging one for me through all the trauma, grief, and heartbreak. But Jesus never left me. He was always with me, holding me during emotional and physical pain and comforting me when I cried out to Him. Jesus reminded me, "The Lord himself goes before you and will be with you; he will never leave you nor forsake you. Do not be afraid; do not be discouraged" (Deuteronomy 31:8, NIV). God continually reminded me that He was not done with me yet. My life could still be used mightily. The Holy Spirit used the pain and suffering in 2020 to make me stronger and more spiritually mature and to prepare me for the next season of my life. God declares to us that "The Lord says, "I will rescue those who love me. I will protect those who trust in my name. When they call on me, I will answer; I will be with them in trouble. I will rescue and honor them" (Psalm 91:14-15, NLT).

Chapter 10

FAVOUR OF THE LORD

*Th*ere are seasons of brokenness and struggle and seasons of victory and success. A time of difficulty can transform into a time of triumph. "To everything there is a season, A time for every purpose under heaven" (Ecclesiastes 3:3, NKJV). When we truly give our lives to the Lord Jesus and obey His guidance, no matter what season we are in, God's favour will be upon us. "May the favor of the Lord our God rest on us; establish the work of our hands for us— yes, establish the work of our hands" (Psalm 90:17, NIV).

The years of 2021 and most of 2022 were excellent because I was doing exceptionally well academically, psychologically, and physically. I have not been in the hospital since November 2020, and the Lord's favour was upon me, which blessed me academically and gave me great wisdom and understanding. In 2020, I was going through the valley of death, but once through it, I arrived on the mountaintop of excitement, joy, and victory. In June 2021, I was preparing for the Master of Counselling program's comprehensive exam. The exam had a written portion and a mock counselling session portion. I was slightly nervous about the comprehensive exam because I lacked practical experience of using counselling skills for the counselling portion of the exam, and I could not start my practicum if I did not pass it.

I did exceptionally well on the written portion of the comprehensive exam and passed. During the counselling portion of the exam, two judges watched my mock counselling session and graded my performance. One of the judges could not hear me well due to my air conditioning and their computer audio loudness. The other judge could hear me clearly and said I had done an excellent job during the mock counselling session. The two judges decided to let me pass the counselling portion of the comprehensive exam. I passed my comprehensive exam. Praise the Lord. Since I passed the comprehensive exam, I could start my practicum in September 2021. "Praise the Lord. Give thanks to the Lord, for he is good; his love endures forever" (Psalm 106:1, NIV).

In July 2021, I started my Master of Counselling capstone project. A capstone project is one level below a thesis paper. I titled my capstone project, *No BodyMind Left Behind*, which was about mental health supports for individuals and families impacted by physical health conditions, Canadian disability history, and disability discrimination. The Master of Counselling capstone project was challenging. It had to be a minimum of fifty pages long, use a mountain of references, research for 100+ hours, and make multiple submissions to a capstone project advisor for revisions. The capstone project had to be completed in one year, which was difficult because it took at least 500 hours to complete while taking other Master of Counselling courses and practicum simultaneously. It was exhausting, but the Lord gave me strength to finish my capstone project. "The Lord gives strength to his people; the Lord blesses his people with peace" (Psalm 29:11, NIV).

I started looking for practicum placement six months before September 2021. It was challenging due to being in the middle of the COVID-19 pandemic. Most practicum placements were taken, and being immune compromised, I could not see clients in person. Eventually, I did find a practicum placement in September 2021, but it was not one I wanted. I was not happy with how I was treated and what I was taught there. The director and two trainers at the practicum placement were unprofessional and unethical and did not correctly follow the professional counselling Code of Ethics or Standards of Practice.

During my practicum placement orientation, the trainer taught us that we should lie to clients if they ask if we are a student counsellor or that we should avoid the question. That trainer's advice was unethical and went against the ethics I learned in the Master of Counselling program. I told my practicum instructor at my school about it, and they were confused about why the trainer was teaching unprofessional, unethical practices. Since I am a person of integrity, I decided to follow the professional counselling code of ethics, so if clients asked if I was a student counsellor, I told them the truth even if the practicum placement did not want me to.

A few of my practicum clients did ask, and I was truthful with them. The director of the practicum placement became angry and asked me more than once, "Why did you tell the client you were a student counsellor?" I ignored it. Following the Counselling Code of Ethics, being ethical, and having integrity was the right thing to do regardless of the consequences. "The Lord detests lying lips, but he delights in those who tell the truth" (Proverbs 12:22, NLT).

I did additional practicum training with another trainer, and they were unprofessional, impolite, and treated me like I was incompetent. Eventually, the trainer was fired because of their unprofessional behaviour toward other people at the practicum site. I put up with the mistreatment because I needed to get my 300 practicum hours completed. My practicum counselling supervisor was responsible for providing me with mentorship, evaluation, and teaching counselling skills. My supervisor listened to or watched my recordings and told me I was a capable student counsellor.

Getting my practicum counselling hours was going well, and I had a fair number of clients at the practicum site. When the provincial COVID-19 restrictions lifted to allow in-person counselling again,

I started to get very few clients. I asked the director about this, and they told me that many of their clients requested one in-person counselling again and I couldn't provide in-person counselling due to health reasons. I asked the director if I could be given the clients who wanted phone or video counselling, but they made minimal effort to accommodate me.

After a while, I realized that the director was discriminating against me and had lied about why I wasn't assigned get more clients. I discovered at group supervision that the other practicum counsellors were getting almost all the clients who wanted video or phone counselling. I confronted the director about it, and they simply told me because I was a young, male counsellor who could not do in-person counselling they couldn't give me very many clients. They clearly were discriminating against my age, gender, disability, and having a health condition. I told my practicum supervisor and practicum instructor about the situation, but they did nothing about it.

I decided to find another practicum placement. In the beginning, looking for another practicum placement was difficult. I had a few interviews, but they did not go well because the interviewers were clearly uncomfortable with my disability, wheelchair, and mouthpiece ventilator. One of the interviewers even told me they could not hire me because my wheelchair and disability would make their clients uncomfortable. The other interviewers made excuses why they could not hire me instead of telling me they were uncomfortable with my wheelchair and disability.

I was shocked at how much hatred and discrimination the mental health field had toward people with disabilities and health conditions. There are many hypocritical people in the counselling field. Counsellors are trained to be empathetic, compassionate, and understanding, but most counsellors do not show these personality qualities to clients or to people with physical disabilities. The most difficult part of having a disability and/or health condition is the discrimination and hatred received from others due to being different.

Despite being discriminated against and rejected repeatedly, it did not stop me from looking for another practicum placement. After being turned down for a few months by many counselling agencies, I eventually got an email reply from a counselling agency director who seemed interested in potentially offering me a practicum placement. The director and I emailed each other back and forth a dozen times, and the director decided to give me a practicum position at their counselling agency.

The amazing thing was that I wasn't even interviewed for the practicum position because they were impressed with my resume, and they noticed my knowledge, wisdom, and understanding acquired from my personal experience of having a disability and health condition. They saw my personal life experience as an asset to the clients I would be counselling. I started being a practicum counsellor at that agency in February 2020. Thank You, Lord! "And my God will meet all your needs according to the riches of his glory in Christ Jesus" (Philippians 4:19, NIV).

I still needed to continue working the previous practicum placement because the new one could not provide enough hours, so I did both practicums simultaneously. It was nice to finally have a placement at an agency whose staff did not discriminate against my disability and who accepted me for who I was. I received a warm welcome from all the co-practicum students and staff, which made me feel like I was part of the agency's community. They even had my back whenever clients mistreated me because of my disability and health condition. I was blessed to have an excellent supervisor whose counselling perspective was similar to mine. I learned a lot from the new supervisor, and I am grateful for their training and friendship. I was accumulating my practicum counselling hours at both practicum sites, and everything was going well at my new practicum placement.

During the spring and summer of 2022, I participated in various disability activism events online. I love being involved in disability activism, fighting discrimination and hatred, and defending the rights of people with disabilities. I engage in disability activism whenever I have the chance. In June 2022, I attended a disability activism focus group on a Zoom meeting for the Canadian Disability Benefit (Federal Disability Income Assistance). The purpose of the focus group was to gather people's thoughts, feelings, and ideas about the proposed Canadian disability benefit and then to write a speech for an NDP politician. Some of my contributions to the focus group I shared were used during the presentation to the House of Commons in Ottawa directed toward Justin Trudeau. It was exciting being involved in political disability activism and that my voice could make a difference.

In the middle of June 2022, I made a presentation at my school's capstone conference on the disability justice movement. Disability justice is a social justice movement that examines disability and ableism and seeks to eliminate ableism and other forms of oppression and identity, such as race, class, and gender. The goal of my presentation was to educate people about disability justice, something barely anybody knows about. Because of God's greatness, my school's faculty and the staff running the conference were amazed by my presentation. They invited me to share my presentation again on another occasion to educate faculty, staff, and students about disability justice. Educating people about disability justice is essential to engaging in it.

At the beginning of June 2020, I learned that the students with disabilities at my school were not getting their accommodations and disability funding because the disability advisor was not adequately trained and educated, making them unqualified to be in that position. It is illegal in Canada, provincially and federally, for postsecondary educational institutes not to provide accommodations and disability funding to students with disabilities according to government outlines. Also, it violated the Canadian Charter of Rights and Freedoms of Equality rights. As a person who engages in disability activism and believes in disability justice, I could not tolerate the oppression of the rights of students with disabilities at my school, so I decided to take action to change this.

I emailed a few administration staff members at my school about the importance of hiring an adequately trained disability advisor, and they told me I needed to talk to somebody in a higher position of power at my school. The only person who had the authority to hire a proper disability advisor was my school's vice president. Determined, I started emailing the vice president about why there needed to be an adequately trained disability advisor, but they kept making excuses as to why they could not hire one.

At first, I tried using gentler and softer disability activism approaches, which did not work, so I had to resort to a strong, assertive approach. Eventually, I told the vice president that if they were unwilling to hire an adequate disability advisor, then the school would be in violation of provincial and federal law, and I let them know the consequences should the school be reported. I persuaded the vice president to get a proper disability advisor.

It was a great victory for disability justice and for the students with disabilities at my school. I was willing to report the school to the government's provincial and federal human rights tribunal and go to the news if I had to. When I pursue justice, I never back down until justice is achieved. "He has shown you, O mortal, what is good. And what does the Lord require of you? To act justly and to love mercy and to walk humbly with your God" (Micah 6:8, NIV). Pursuing justice fills me with excitement and passion to fight back against oppression. There is joy for those who deal justly with others and always do what is right (Psalm 106:3). The Lord blesses people who fight against oppression, pursue justice, and do what is right.

Chapter 11

GOD IS MY REFUGE AND STRENGTH

There are times in life when we are unsure if we will make it, and our strength starts failing physically and/or mentally. We can choose to give up in defeat or keep trying until we triumph. When Jesus is in our hearts, we can rely on Him as our refuge and strength in times of difficulty, sadness, and fear. Indeed, He will comfort us and help us overcome our challenging situations. "God is our refuge and strength, an ever-present help in trouble" (Psalm 46:1, NIV).

On Thursday, July 7, 2022, I began experiencing severe stomach and right-side pain with nausea and multiple bowel movements. The pain was so unbearable I had to go to the hospital Emergency Department to manage my pain with a hydromorphone injection and then to figure out what was causing my severe pain. I had to wait almost four hours to receive a hydromorphone injection for the pain because the emergency nurse did not believe I was in severe pain, so they made me wait to see the doctor first.

The emergency doctor arrived and began a physical exam with their hands, putting pressure and feeling my digestive system organs. When the doctor pressed on the area where my liver and gallbladder were, and I let out a shout of pain. They ordered an abdominal ultrasound and an injection of hydromorphone for the pain. A few minutes after receiving my hydromorphone injection, my pain was reduced significantly. The abdominal ultrasound did not provide the emergency doctor with any useful information. I was still in a lot of pain when my hydromorphone injection started to wear off, so the doctor ordered an abdominal CT scan to get a clear image of what was causing my abdominal pain. A few hours after the CT scan, the doctor told me I had a five-millimetre gallstone stuck in my bile duct. The emergency doctor admitted me to the hospital because stuck gallstones cause severe pain, liver dysfunction and damage, and can cause a life-threatening acute gallbladder infection.

After being at the hospital for two days, my liver started failing, causing jaundice (yellowing of the skin and eyes), and I started developing an acute gallbladder infection. The gastroenterologist told me that, due to my Duchenne muscular dystrophy, there was a 50% chance I would die if I had gallbladder removal surgery, and if I did not get surgery, there was a much higher chance I would die from the gallbladder infection. The medical team decided to stall and give me IV antibiotics for the gallbladder infection, hoping the gallstone would pass through the bile duct by itself. The medical team determined I had to be sicker to justify getting a high-risk surgery and hoped I would not get sepsis. Sepsis, also called blood poisoning, is a life-threatening immune response to a blood infection.

Two days later, it became obvious that my body was losing the battle against the gallbladder infection. It was spreading, and I entered the first stage of sepsis. The doctors were very concerned that I was going to die from sepsis. Out of fear and desperation, knowing I likely would die, I turned to God by listening and singing worship healing songs and praying to God with all my might, heart, and soul. I knew that Jesus was the only one with the power to save me from death. Jesus had saved me multiple times before when I had pneumonia and collapsed lungs, so I had faith that Jesus could save me from death again.

One night in my hospital room, I was listening and singing healing worship songs and praying, pouring out my heart to God when the fire of the Holy Spirit touched me, and God whispered to me, "Do not worry, My son. Do not worry, My son." When I heard those words, I started to cry, because I knew Jesus would rescue me from death and heal me, and I knew everything would be alright. After that night, God started doing miracles. The gallstone exited my bile duct, my body won the battle against infection, sepsis disappeared, and my liver returned to normal functioning.

The doctor told me, "I thought you were going to die, because healthy young adults with out your health conditions usually die from acute gallbladder infections and sepsis." The doctor could not understand how I was still alive. Looking confused, the doctor said, "I do not know what you did, but it worked."

It was medically impossible for me to survive an acute gallbladder infection and sepsis while immunocompromised, but through God, impossible things became possible. Six days later, I was released from the hospital and went home. "The LORD says, 'I will rescue those who love me. I will protect those who trust in my name. When they call on me, I will answer; I will be with them in trouble. I will rescue and honor them'" (Psalm 91:14-15, NLT). In times of crisis or impossible situations, Jesus is close to our hearts to provide us comfort and peace. In desperate situations, seek the Lord, cry out in prayer, and He will provide a way out of the situation. The things that seem impossible to humans are possible for God, because He is the God of the impossible.

Since 2020, my father was in end-stage Parkinson's disease, which caused him significant muscle pain, difficulty eating and speaking, significant memory loss, dementia, difficulty breathing, and the inability to care for himself in any capacity, requiring 24-hour caregiving. I visited my father with Jeanilyn once a month even though it was dangerous for me due to being immunocompromised, but I thought it was worth the risk. It was painful to me to see my father die slowly with significant physical pain and becoming increasingly thinner until he could see his own bones clearly.

In 2022, my father was in and out of the hospital with sepsis because he could no longer verbally communicate symptoms of infections. Two months before my father's death, I and Jeanilyn visited him and asked if he would like to accept Jesus as his Lord and personal Saviour. My father looked at me, mumbled yes and grabbed my hand. Then, Jeanilyn and I prayed with my father, allowing him an opportunity to accept Jesus as his Lord and personal Saviour. Only God knows if my father truly accepted Jesus into his heart and if he is in Heaven now. I hope he did, but if not, he will spend eternity suffering in hell, which would be heartbreaking. God is extremely clear: "If you declare with your mouth, 'Jesus is Lord,' and believe in your heart that God raised him from the dead, you will be saved. For it is with your heart that you believe and are justified, and it is with your mouth that you profess your faith and are saved" (Romans 10:9-10, NIV). If Jesus is not or no longer your Lord and personal Saviour when you die, you will spend eternity in hell because you chose not to give your life to Jesus. God gave us freewill to choose. It is your choice to decide where you want to spend your eternity. I am telling you this because I love you and do not want you to spend eternity in hell.

Two weeks before my father's death, the Holy Spirit kept urging me to visit my father. A week before my father's death, I visited him for the last time, told him that I loved him, thanked him for everything he had done for me, and said goodbye because I felt this was the last time I would see him. A week later, I received a phone call from my older brother that our father had died.

My father died on August 13, 2022. I was not surprised when my brother called with the news because the Holy Spirit had informed me that my father would die soon. My initial reaction to hearing the news of my father's death was relief that my father was no longer suffering and a little bit sad at the same time. I am grateful that God allowed me to have a meaningful last visit and to say goodbye to my father. My father's celebration of life was on August 22, 2022. I enjoyed hearing stories of my father's life that I did not know about. When I heard speeches about how proud my father was of me and my brothers, I would get teary-eyed, knowing my father had made it clear to everybody that he was proud of us and loved us when he was alive.

On August 30, 2022, I went to the hospital's Emergency Department because I was having severe gallbladder pain again. I was given a hydromorphone injection and sent home that day with the hospital At-Home program following up with me at my home a few times a day. Each day, the hospital At-Home doctor and their colleague would come to my house three times a day to do blood tests, perform a check-up, and give me a hydromorphone injection if needed.

But two days later, a blood test indicated that I had significant inflammation and probably a serious gallbladder infection. The At-Home Doctor told me I needed to return to the hospital to be admitted because I was very sick. On September 1, 2022, I returned to the hospital to be admitted. The emergency doctor ordered some blood tests and an abdominal ultrasound of my liver and gallbladder to see if I had another gallstone stuck in the bile duct. I did. In fact, I had a large gallstone stuck in the bile duct along with a severe infection. This time, the gallstone was too large to pass through the bile duct by itself, and the doctor said I had to have gallbladder removal surgery to survive or the gallbladder infection would eventually kill me. Without surgery, my gallbladder would keep filling up with bacteria and bile until it exploded, spreading toxic bacteria that would cause me to die from sepsis. Lastly, they told me that due to compromised breathing and impaired heart function, there was a 50% chance I would not survive the surgery. My respirologist told me I would be intimated (a tube inserted through the mouth then down into trachea to help you breathe) and put on a breathing machine while being kept asleep for two days after the surgery. For the next four days, the medical and surgical teams and my respirologists carefully planned my surgery because of how risky it would be for me.

My gallbladder removal surgery was scheduled for September 4, but I told the general surgeon that I would like to postpone by one day. I did not want to ruin Janella's fourth birthday party. Due to the rescheduling, a different general surgeon was assigned to do my surgery. This turned out to be a blessing, because the new surgeon was very kind and was known to be one of the best surgeons in my city. God wanted me to have the best surgeon I could get. "The Lord will indeed give what is good, and our land will yield its harvest" (Psalm 85:12, NIV). The two days before my gallbladder removal surgery, I became extremely anxious because there was a 50% chance of dying during the surgery, and the idea of a tube being down my throat and in my trachea didn't help either.

The night before my surgery, I was with Jeanilyn, when a brother and sister in Christ Jesus visited me to pray with me for God's intervention during surgery, and that I would wake up from anesthesia. The rest of my local church also prayed for my surgery. On the morning of September 5, Jeanilyn, her sister Myrna, and some medical staff brought me to the operating room. On the way, I trembled in fear, knowing that moment could be one of the last ones of my life. In the operating room, the general surgeon asked me some questions and moved my head around to plan how the intubation tube would be placed. Soon after, the surgeon was done with their assessment, Jeanilyn, Myrna, and the surgical team transferred me onto the operating table and helped me into a comfortable position for the surgery. After that, Jeanilyn and Myrna had to say goodbye and leave. That was the most uncomfortable and stressful goodbye I have ever experienced. It could have been our last goodbye.

After Jeanilyn and Myrna left, the general surgeon asked, "Are you ready for us to start the surgery?"

I answered, "Yes."

Then the anaesthesiologist told me the anesthesia medication they would inject into my IV would burn a lot. They asked me again if I was ready, and I said yes. When they injected the anesthetic medication, I felt an excruciating burning feeling in my vein where the IV was. Ten seconds later, I fell unconscious.

A few life-threatening complications occurred during my gallbladder removal surgery, which dramatically decreased the probability that I would survive the surgery. The surgery was supposed to take forty minutes but took four hours due to the anaesthesiologist accidentally puncturing my left lung when inserting the central line in a major vein. I lost a litre of blood and a collapsed lung. Also, the position I was lying made it awkward for the surgeon to remove my gallbladder. Because of God's greatness and the prayers of Jeanilyn, her family, and all my brothers and sisters in Christ, I survived the gallbladder removal surgery and woke up two days later.

I woke up in a lot of pain, felt nauseous, confused, dizzy, and had blurred vision due to the anesthesia medication, blood loss, and low minerals in my blood. The scariest and most challenging part of recovering from surgery was learning how to swallow again without choking.

A few days after waking up from the surgery, the surgeon came to my ICU room for a checkup. The surgeon explained that my gallbladder had been extremely swollen, like a balloon, and had to be removed cautiously to keep it from exploding. They told me that if I had had my gallbladder removal surgery six hours later, my gallbladder would have exploded, and I would have died from bacterial blood poisoning (sepsis) from the gallbladder infection. Finally, the surgeon told me I had a three-centimeter (the size of a small strawberry) gallstone stuck in my gallbladder duct.

Without God's protection and the prayers of others, I would have died in surgery or not have woken up from anesthesia. God gave me deliverance, and it is a miracle that I am alive. I felt so blessed by all my brothers and sisters in Christ who prayed for me, and by God who provided me with one of the top-rated general surgeons to do my surgery. God is so good that he never leaves me in times of great fear and comforts me when I am afraid. While recovering from my surgery, I spent time with the Lord Jesus, singing praise and worship songs; I often cried because I was reminded of God's love, goodness in my life, and His faithfulness. Through this experience, I have witnessed God's deliverance, greatness, and goodness. Surviving and recovering from the surgery made me realize how good God is, that life is a gift, and that there is nothing too difficult for the Lord.

During our darkest and scariest moments in life, the Lord is always with us, "So do not fear, for I am with you; do not be dismayed, for I am your God. I will strengthen you and help you; I will uphold you with my righteous right hand" (Isaiah 41:10, NIV). Sometimes, life gets difficult, but the Lord strengthens us and helps us overcome challenging life circumstances. The Lord is always with us and never abandons us because "The Lord himself goes before you and will be with you; he will never leave you nor forsake you. Do not be afraid; do not be discouraged" (Deuteronomy 31:8, NIV).

Chapter 12

PROSPERITY IN THE LORD

When we have a close personal relationship with the Lord Jesus, He will prosper us financially and educationally and with wisdom and good health. "And this same God who takes care of me will supply all your needs from his glorious riches, which have been given to us in Christ Jesus" (Philippians 4:19, NLT). The Lord will greatly bless our lives when we obey God and follow His plan. When we disobey the Lord's plan for our lives, life becomes difficult, and we struggle in every aspect. Since God gave us freewill, it is our choice whether we want to be richly blessed or not.

After fifteen months of research, writing, and many revisions and corrections from my capstone project advisor, I finally completed my Master's Capstone Project in October 2022. Completing the capstone project was hard work, but I was pleased with how it turned out. After doing 100-plus hours of research, I became an expert in physical disability counselling, physical health condition counselling, and disability justice counselling. I am one of the very few people in Canada who specialize in those types of counselling therapies.

In December 2022, I sent my resignation letter to the director of my first practicum site. I resigned due to the constant discrimination and being given barely any clients, which was not worth sacrificing my mental health for. I am grateful that some of my school's faculty members and the director of the Master Counselling program helped me to find a new practicum placement to replace the one I resigned from. In January 2023, I started a third practicum at my school's counselling clinic. For the rest of my Master of Counselling practicum, I continued at my second and third practicum sites until I completed my practicum hours. My second practicum site said they would offer me a job when I completed my Master of Counselling program. I felt incredibly blessed and relieved by this. I knew it would be challenging to get a job elsewhere due to discrimination toward people with disabilities in the counselling field.

After ten years of post-secondary education, I finally attained my Master of Counselling diploma in June 2023. Since I graduated, I could now be called a mental health expert and put the initials MC at the end of my name. I would never have gotten my Master of Counselling degree without the help and support of God, my father, my mother, my family, Jeanilyn, my Filipino family, and tutor. Once I received my physical diploma, I accepted the job offered by the director of the second practicum site. I started work as a therapeutic counsellor in June of 2023 at their counselling agency. As far as I know, I became the first counsellor in the province of British Columbia who has a Master of Counselling degree and specializes in physical disability counselling, physical health condition counselling, and disability justice counselling.

At the end of June 2023, I applied for my registered clinical counsellor (RCC) and Canadian certified counsellor (CCC) designations. Once I receive my RCC and/or CCC, the agency I work for will significantly increase my pay and give me a larger client load. In addition, clients can use their extended medical insurance coverage to pay my counselling fees, attracting even more clients to work with. Finally, after twelve years, I had the opportunity to get out of poverty.

When I am blessed with financially stability, I want to share my wealth with the poor and people less fortunate than me. When you bless people who are poor or in need, you fill their lives with joy and hope, which blesses you with joy and happiness. I once gave $50 to buy groceries for poor families in Jeanilyn's home village in the Philippines during Easter. Jeanilyn's family in the Philippines took a video showing the gratitude of those I'd helped. When I saw how happy and grateful those families were, I cried tears of joy that I was able to make their Easter holidays special to them. "In everything I did, I showed you that by this kind of hard work we must help the weak, remembering the words the Lord Jesus himself said: 'It is more blessed to give than to receive'" (Acts 20:35, NIV). When people are greedy with their wealth and do not share it with others, they do not have satisfaction and joy in their lives. "Then he said, 'Beware! Guard against every kind of greed. Life is not measured by how much you own'" (Luke 12:15, NLT). Being greedy is not suitable for humans because it eventually makes them physically and mentally sick due to working excessively to get rich.

CONCLUSION

Everyone's life is worth living, no matter what circumstance you were born into or are currently in. Your life has a purpose. Nobody was ever born a mistake, because God makes every individual perfect without exception. "For you created my inmost being; you knit me together in my mother's womb. I praise you because I am fearfully and wonderfully made; your works are wonderful, I know that full well" (Psalm 139:13-14, NIV).

Every life is beautiful, regardless of whether you were born with an illness, developed an illness, have a disability, or have a short life. Life is a blessing from God that we often forget to appreciate, especially when we experience seasons of pain.

I have been through many seasons in my life that I thought I would not make it through, sometimes even to the point of death. While in other seasons, I was on the mountaintops of victory and joy. There are many seasons in life where there is a time to cry and a time to laugh, a time to grieve, and a time to dance (Ecclesiastes 3:4, NLT). Through it all, God was faithful, was so good to me, never abandoned or forsook me, and was always by my side. He always provided a way when there seemed to be no way. No matter how dark our situation may seem, there is nothing God cannot help us overcome, even if we are facing depression, sickness, disease, or grief and loss.

I have witnessed God do impossible things in my life that are beyond human understanding. God can bring miracles in your life and help you have a powerful, impactful life, but only if you surrender your life to the Lord Jesus and trust in Him. If you have not given your life to Jesus and serve God, you are not truly alive, and life will have no meaning or purpose.

My life is a testimony that God is a real person. All the miracles God has done in my life defy human wisdom and make it impossible to deny the existence of God.

I hope this book will help you decide to give your life to Jesus and to let Him become your Lord and personal Saviour. Jesus is waiting for you to accept Him so He can embrace you and tell you He loves you so much. Giving your life to Jesus is the most wonderful decision you can make in your life, one you will never regret. I want you to experience the love of God in your life as I have experienced it. Money, success, status, material possessions, or religion can not fill the hole in your heart. Jesus is the only one who can fill the void in our hearts. When you accept Jesus, God promises, "Now may the God of hope fill you with all joy and peace in believing, that you may abound in hope by the power of the Holy Spirit" (Romans 15:13, NKJV).

To all the brothers and sisters in Christ who read this book, I hope it helps you give your life to Jesus or strengthens you and encourages you to continue the good fight of faith or to return to the path God wants you to walk. I love you with the love of the Lord, and I hope my story blessed your life.

Printed in the United States
by Baker & Taylor Publisher Services